THE COOLEST CHINESE Martial Arts

Amy Holt

CRAZY COOL CHINA

ROSEN PUBLISHING
NEW YORK

SinolinguA
华语教学出版社
BEIJING

Published in 2023 by The Rosen Publishing Group, Inc.
2544 Clinton Street, Buffalo, NY 14224

Jointly published in 2023 by Sinolingua Co.,Ltd., Beijing, China, and The Rosen Publishing Group, Inc., New York, New York, United States.

First Edition

Editor: Jennifer Lombardo
Designer: Rachel Rising

Photo credits: Cover, Grekov's/Shutterstock.com; cover, pp. 1-48 Sylfida/Shutterstock.com; pp. 4, 6, 10, 14, 18, 22, 26, 30, 34, 38, 40 Attl Tibor/Shutterstock.com; p. 5 TuiPhotoEngineer/Shutterstock.com; p. 7 Shan_shan/Shutterstock.com–; p. 8 https://commons.wikimedia.org/wiki/File:Shuaijiao_taizhou_jiangsu_2007_11_24_IMG_2871.JPG; p. 11 Shahril KHMD/Shutterstock.com; p. 12 Daniel Andis/Shutterstock.com; p. 15 Skreidzeleu/Shutterstock.com; p. 16 xian-photos/Shutterstock.com; p. 19 Dan_Koleska/Shutterstock.com; p. 19 Rejean Aline Bedard/Shutterstock.com; p. 20 Take A Pix Media/Shutterstock.com; p. 23 Olga L Galkina/Shutterstock.com; p. 24 https://commons.wikimedia.org/wiki/File:Ip_Man_Memorial_Hall_@_Luo_Village_09.jpg. p. 27 Koyurik/Shutterstock.com; p. 28 Shahjehan/Shutterstock.com; p. 31, 35 CHEN WS/Shutterstock.com; p. 32 https://commons.wikimedia.org/wiki/File:Deerhornknives.JPG; p. 36 UfaBizPhoto/Shutterstock.com; p. 39 ilapinto/Shutterstock.com; p. 40 Tinseltown/Shutterstock.com; p. 43 BearFotos/Shutterstock.com.

Cataloging-in-Publication Data

Names: Holt, Amy
Title: The coolest chinese martial arts / Amy Holt.
Description: New York : Rosen Publishing, 2023. | Series: Crazy Cool China | Includes bibliographic information, glossary and index.
Identifiers: ISBN 9781499474633 (pbk) | ISBN 9781499474640 (library bound) | ISBN 9781499474657 (ebook)
Subjects: LCSH: Hand-to-hand fighting, Oriental– Juvenile literature | Martial arts– Juvenile literature
Classification: LCC GV1101.35 H65 2023 | DDC 796.815 -dc23

Manufactured in the United States of America

CPSIA Compliance Information: Batch #CW23. For further information, contact Rosen Publishing, New York, New York, at 1-800-237-9932.

Contents

WHAT ARE MARTIAL ARTS? 4
CHINA'S MARTIAL ARTS HISTORY 6
GROUPING THE MARTIAL ARTS 10
KUNG FU 14
TAI CHI 18
WING CHUN 22
CHANGQUAN 26
BAGUAZHANG 30
SANDA 34
MARTIAL ARTS IN FILM 38
DON'T GET IT TWISTED! 42
GLOSSARY 44
FOR MORE INFORMATION 45
FOR FURTHER READING 46
BIBLIOGRAPHY 47
INDEX 48

What Are Martial Arts?

Humans have invented all kinds of weapons over the course of history. Arrows, guns, swords, and spears are just a few of the tools people can use to defend themselves. However, the human body itself can also be a weapon—with the correct training.

Martial arts are also great for improving a person's **self-confidence**. One reason for this is that knowing they have a way to defend themselves if they need to makes them feel stronger. Another is that becoming good at any kind of skill makes people feel good about themselves.

Although martial arts were created to weaponize the human body—the word "martial" means "relating to war"—there are a variety of other reasons why people practice them. One is for exercise. Any kind of fighting is good exercise because it works all the muscles of the body and gets the heart pumping. Another reason why people may choose to practice a martial art is to make new friends. Classes get people out of the house and introduce them to people they might otherwise never have met. While many different cultures have created their own forms of martial arts, Chinese martial arts are some of the oldest forms in human history.

A trained martial artist can move their body in incredible ways!

China's Martial Arts History

China is one of the oldest countries in the world. It is so old, in fact, that many parts of its history and culture were developed before they started keeping written records. Chinese martial arts are one such area. They are believed to have started about 4,000 years ago—a time without many written records. Without written information available, there is no way to be sure who created martial arts or why.

During the long course of Chinese history, travelers to and from China brought Chinese martial arts to many different places around the world.

The best guess about how martial arts developed is that people started fighting in self-defense. Over time, fighting styles were **systematized** and used mainly by the military.

A significant number of written records started to emerge during the Shang dynasty. Shown here is a Shang-era record written on a tortoise shell.

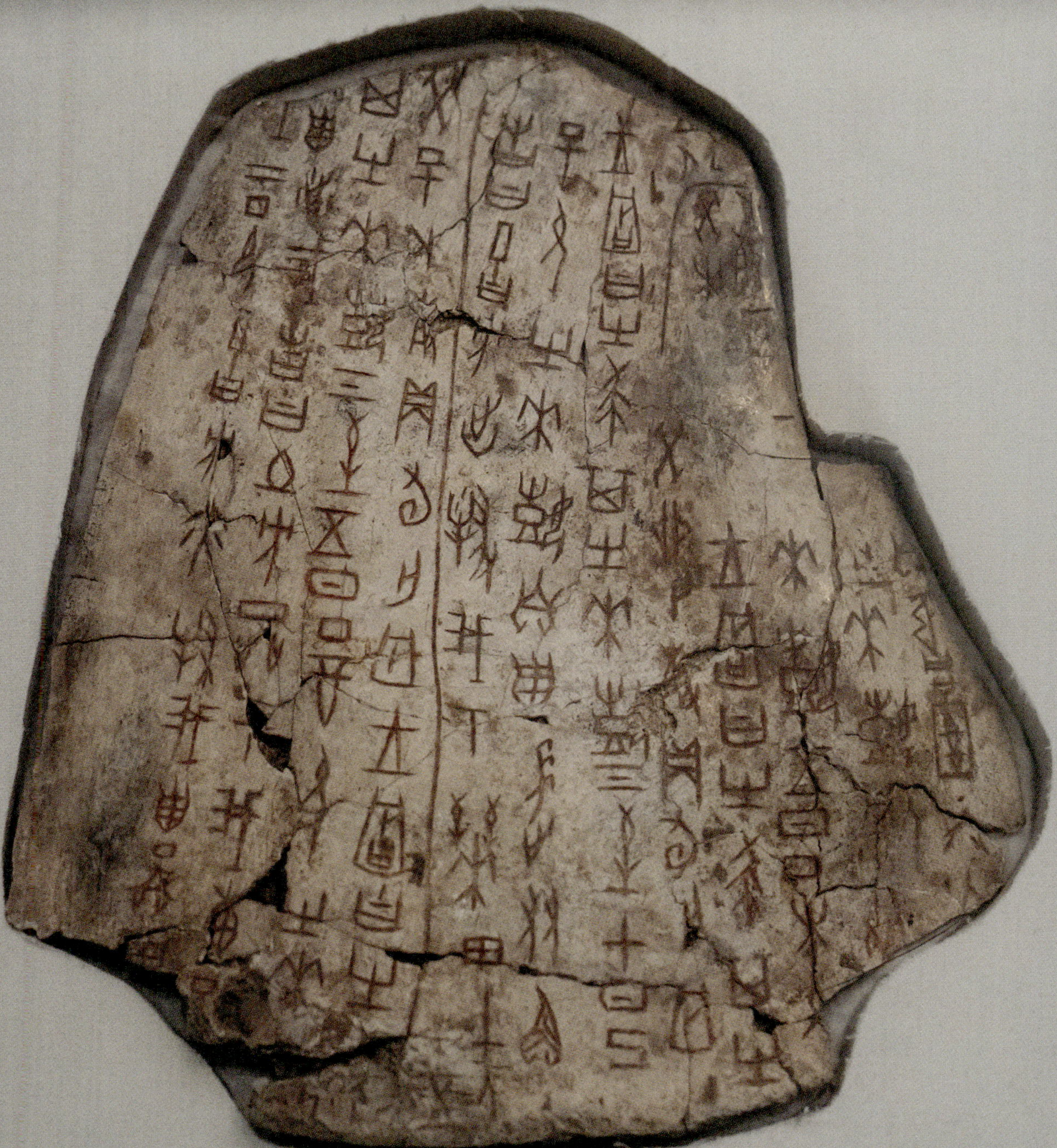

These two men are wearing Shuai Jiao uniforms.

Different groups created their own schools, or kinds, of Shuai Jiao. For example, the Mongolian, the Uygur, and the Yi are three minority ethnic groups that each have their own styles. Other styles of Shuai Jiao include Beijing, Tianjin, and Baoding.

Around 200 BCE, it is believed the martial arts became a sport that people outside the military could practice. They would fight to show off their skill rather than to seriously hurt their opponent. The best competitors were often chosen to guard the emperor. One of the early forms of martial arts is called Jue Li. The name later changed to Shuai Jiao, and this is the name by which it is known today. When people practice Shuai Jiao, they usually wear a jacket with short sleeves and a loose-fitting pair of pants. In competitions, points are awarded for both the style and effectiveness of the moves.

Shuai Jiao provided a foundation for some Chinese martial arts. Some styles combined dance moves with attack moves, turning martial arts into both a method of self-defense and an art form. Some include weapons such as spears, while others use only the human body. The different martial arts can be grouped into several different categories, depending on what criteria are being used.

Grouping the Martial Arts

The two main groups of martial arts are "external" styles and "internal" styles. These are also sometimes called "hard" and "soft" styles. External, meaning outside, focuses on using the body's muscles to make fast, graceful movements. Often, people will yell or growl while practicing an external style of martial arts. These are the styles people often think of as being used for self-defense.

"Yin" and "yang" are Chinese words used to describe balance in all things. Yin is associated with the mind, darkness, and femininity. Yang is associated with the body, light, and masculinity. Internal martial arts have more yin, and external martial arts have more yang, but both are needed.

Internal, meaning inside, focuses on having control over the body's movements and staying relaxed. Practitioners pay attention to their breathing and their thoughts. The movements in this style are often slower, and these styles are generally what people think of as being used for relaxation.

These kinds of moves are more common in the northern Chinese martial arts.

Because there are a lot of Chinese martial arts that all have slightly different styles—many of which combine some aspects, or parts, of multiple categories—some people think it's pointless to try to categorize them at all.

Not everyone agrees with grouping martial arts this way because most styles use a combination of both. Some people prefer to group the martial arts according to whether they were developed in the north or south of China. The northern style involves a lot of high kicks and **acrobatics**. In the southern style, practitioners get much closer to their opponent, meaning their strikes tend to be faster and lower.

Several words are used to describe Chinese martial arts. Wushu means martial arts in general. Kung fu is often used to describe the use of martial arts outside the military, such as the more artistic styles.

This symbol represents yinyang. It shows how the two ideas connect to make a whole and how each one has a bit of the other inside it.

Kung Fu

Kung fu is an umbrella term, which means it covers a lot of different things. All Chinese martial arts are a type of kung fu. However, when people talk about kung fu, they often mean one specific kind. This kind is called Shaolin kung fu.

Shaolin kung fu gets its name from where it was developed: a **monastery** called the Shaolin Temple in Henan, China. However, like the story of Shuai Jiao, a lot of the facts about the creation of Shaolin kung fu are hidden in legend. People say that a **Buddhist** monk named Bodhidharma came from India to visit the Shaolin Temple and noticed that the monks who lived there were not in very good shape. He created a set of exercises to help them stay fit.

"Kung fu" can be used to describe things that have nothing to do with martial arts. The word translates roughly to "hard work." Anything a person works hard to master can be called "kung fu."

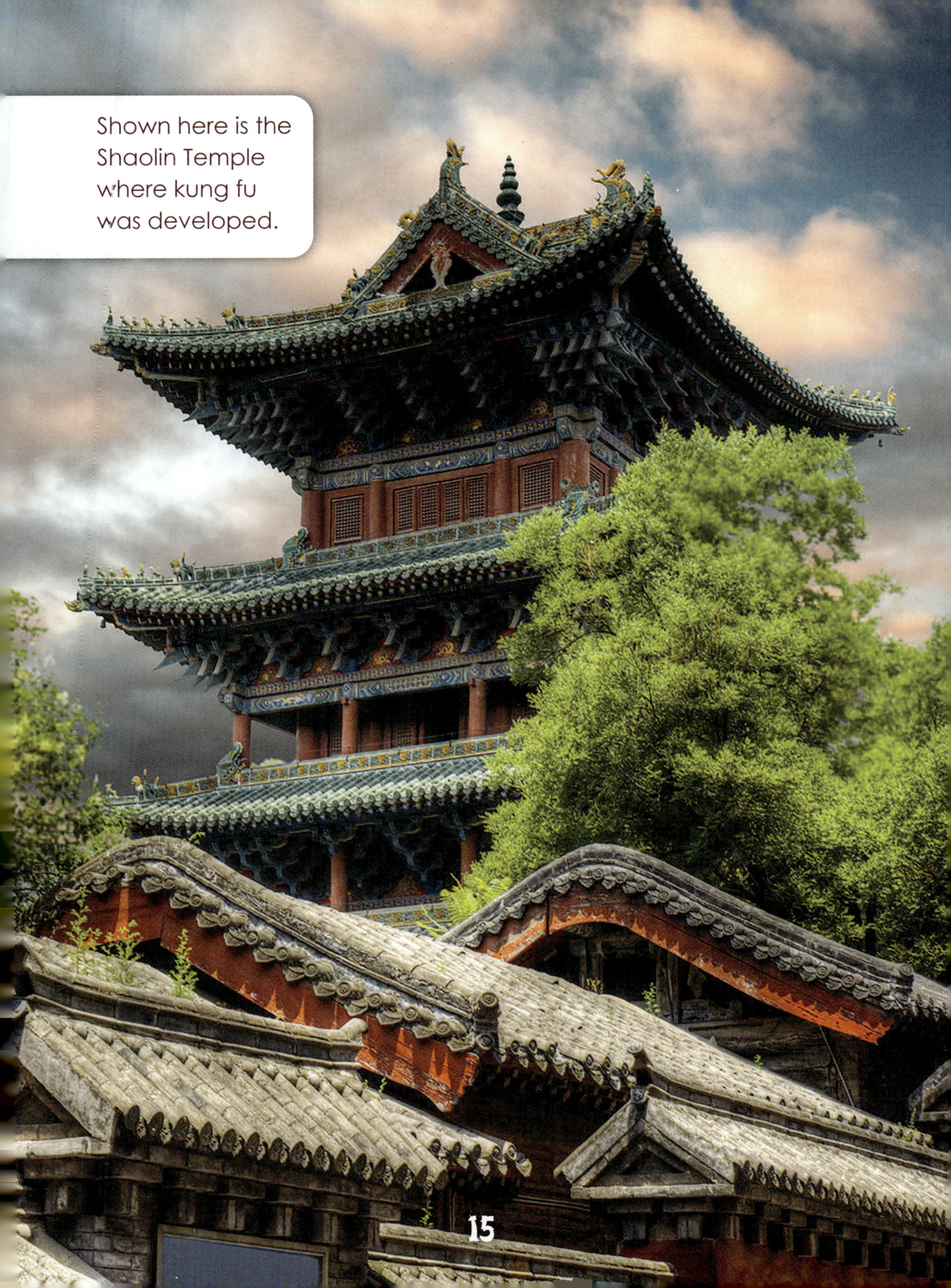

Shown here is the Shaolin Temple where kung fu was developed.

These monks are showing off their kung fu skills for tourists.

In 2008, Dreamworks released the movie *Kung Fu Panda*. It became very popular and showed American kids what the process of learning kung fu might look like. The Furious Five in the movie represent different kung fu fighting styles, such as tiger style and monkey style.

A lot of the monks had been in the Chinese military before they joined the monastery, so they added some martial arts moves to the exercises.

Because the monks were Buddhist, they followed a code of **ethics** when they practiced kung fu. They were not allowed to use their skills to hurt anyone, except in self-defense, and they could not ignore someone else who was being hurt when they had the ability to step in and keep that person safe. A good kung fu practitioner was expected to be honest, fair, cooperative, and respectful at all times—even when they were not fighting.

Shaolin kung fu quickly became the most popular martial arts school in China. It is also one of the styles people outside the country are most familiar with. People who take Shaolin kung fu classes learn the code of ethics as well as the movements.

Tai Chi

While Shaolin kung fu is a more external kind of martial art, tai chi is a more internal one. Tai chi is tied to a **philosophy** called Taoism, which focuses on balancing yin and yang in all things. The origins of tai chi are as mythical as the origins of other Chinese martial arts. Stories say a Taoist priest named Zhang San Feng once saw a fight between a snake and a type of bird called a crane. He used their movements to create a new martial art.

People who follow Taoism say it's impossible to describe in words. In general, they try to avoid conflict, live a simple life that balances yin and yang, and enjoy nature. Huangdi is credited with inventing Taoism, but the most famous Taoist was named Lao-tzu.

Historians tell a different story. They say historical evidence suggests that a man named Chen Wang Ting created tai chi by mixing together his military martial arts experience and Taoist yoga. It was designed for both self-defense and relaxation. Later, people changed Chen Wang Ting's tai chi a little bit, and now there are five kinds. They're called Chen, Yang, Wu, Sun, and Woo.

Legend says tai chi was inspired by a fight between these two creatures.

People don't need special clothes or equipment to practice tai chi.

Tai chi is most frequently done slowly, but there are fast styles, too. There are also some that use weapons. Every tai chi master teaches the art a little bit differently, so there are more than 108 moves that practitioners can do.

Like other martial arts, tai chi has become popular as a form of exercise. Practitioners perform slow, graceful movements that flow into each other. They pay careful attention to their breath and their thoughts. Many people say this makes it relaxing. Because it is slow moving, it's especially good exercise for older adults or other people who have health and **mobility** problems. Practitioners don't fight each other; instead, they stand in rows and all do the same movements at the same time, following along with an instructor.

Tai chi is very popular in China, and its popularity has grown around the world as well. In big cities, it isn't uncommon to see tai chi classes taking place in a park or city center. However, it can also be done alone.

Wing Chun

Like kung fu, wing chun was created at the Shaolin Temple. Its legendary creator—a Buddhist nun named Ng Mui—wanted to make a fighting style that anyone could use, even if they weren't very strong. She changed some of the kung fu moves to create her new martial art. Wing chun makes it easier for smaller people to defend themselves by using an opponent's size and strength against them. Legend says that Ng Mui created her martial art for the woman she named it after: Yim Wing Chun. Ng Mui did this to help Yim Wing Chun get rid of a man she didn't like who wouldn't leave her alone.

> Ip Man is the name of a wing chun grandmaster, or expert. He is credited with making wing chun more widely known and with teaching famous martial artists such as Bruce Lee.

Shaolin kung fu has become an art form that is more commonly practiced for show or for exercise.

However, wing chun is still used by many people as a form of self-defense. For this reason, wing chun movements focus on causing an attacker as much pain as possible to give the person being attacked a chance to get away.

Wing chun fighters get closer to each other than kung fu fighters do.

This statue was made to honor Ip Man after his death.

In 1980, three English men formed a band they named Wang Chung. This sounds similar to wing chun, but they're actually very different words. "Wang chung" in Chinese means "yellow bell." It is the first note in the Chinese classical music scale.

Wing chun movements focus on maintaining balance and moving in close to an opponent to attack them. Some movements can be done with weapons in hand. There are also mental exercises that practitioners use to help them stay aware of what's going on around them. The idea is to help the body develop automatic **reflexes** that can kick in before a person **consciously** realizes they're in danger.

Today, there are 11 main schools of wing chun. They are called Ip Man, Yiu Choi, Jiu Wan, Gulao Village, Pan Nam, Yuen Kay Shan, Nguyen Te-Cong, Cho Family, Hung Fa Yi, Pao Fa Lien, and Fut Sao. Each one has a different style.

Changquan

The name "changquan" translates to "long fist." It is an external fighting style from northern China. It is **characterized** by running, leaping, and performing acrobatic moves. Like Shaolin kung fu, the movements keep the fighters relatively far apart, so a lot of room is needed to perform this martial art.

Since 1991, practitioners of changquan and other martial arts have come together **biennially** to show off their skills at the World Wushu Championships. The event is held in a different place each year. In 2023, it will be held in Fort Worth, Texas.

Because Chinese historians kept careful records in later years, we know that changquan was created by Zhao Kuangyin, the first emperor of the Song Dynasty. He put his own spin on some of the Shaolin kung fu movements to create the style that is now known as changquan.

Many people who practice changquan believe

in attacking before their opponent can do the same. However, some changquan practitioners believe in focusing on defense, not offense. Although changquan can be used for self-defense, the moves are most often done for show in competitions. Unlike some other Chinese martial arts, changquan is practiced without weapons. To be a good changquan fighter, a person needs speed, **accuracy**, and flexibility.

Paper money and gunpowder were two other things invented during the Song Dynasty.

There are several different types of changquan. One of them, which is called chaquan, was developed by Chinese Muslims. Their moves formed the basis for the modern version of changquan that is practiced today.

Changquan is not as commonly practiced as other Chinese martial arts, especially in the West. For example, other martial arts have been added to the Olympic Games, but changquan has not. However, it is a category in the Asian Games, which are similar to the Olympic Games but are attended only by Asian countries. Since 1990, the only time China has not won the gold medal for changquan at the Asian Games was in 2014.

Splits, somersaults, and flying leaps are common moves in changquan.

Baguazhang

A man named Dong Haichuan created baguazhang in the 19th century. He combined several types of martial arts with Taoist circle walking. This is when a person walks in a circle repeatedly as a form of **meditation**. Like tai chi, baguazhang is practiced mainly for physical and mental exercise. There are several different specific ways people can walk the circle. For example, in the mud-walking style, people step high as if they are walking through thick mud.

Baguazhang, tai chi, and another martial art called xingyiquan are the three main martial arts that belong to the Wudang School. This school focuses on internal martial arts rather than external ones.

When people practice baguazhang with another person, they use circular motions combined with kicks and punches to bring their opponent down. This movement style is effective for fighting multiple people at once. By walking in a circle, practitioners can see more of what is going on around them and strike in multiple directions very quickly. Like wing chun, hand strikes are more commonly used than foot strikes in baguazhang, so it is more of a close-range fighting style.

Shown here is an athlete named Joanna Lim showing her baguazhang skills at the 2015 World Wushu Championships.

There is some disagreement about why baguazhang was created. Some say it was intended mainly for exercise. Others say it was meant to help people fight multiple attackers at once, as the circular movements would help a practitioner see all around them and strike in multiple directions quickly.

Baguazhang is sometimes practiced with weapons. During the Qing Dynasty, the emperor's bodyguards were trained in baguazhang. They hid small weapons under their clothes that they could easily pull out if danger arose. These included things such as iron fans and brass knuckles. Some baguazhang practitioners also use very long weapons, such as swords or spears. It is sometimes said that people who are trained in baguazhang are skilled at turning just about anything into a weapon.

Deer horn knives such as these are commonly used baguazhang weapons.

Sanda

Sanda is sometimes called "Chinese kickboxing." Many people don't realize sanda is a Chinese martial art because it looks like a combination of kickboxing and wrestling. Instead of the graceful, dancing movements of many other martial arts, sanda movements tend to be quick and **brutal**.

Sanda clubs can be found all over China. These are gyms where people train to compete in national and international tournaments. Some sanda clubs also teach MMA, boxing, and a Japanese martial art called judo.

Many people believe sanda developed from lei tai arena fights, which were held in ancient China up through the early 1900s. In these fights, participants were allowed to do just about anything to win. A winner would stay in the ring, meeting new challengers until either someone beat them or people gave up challenging them.

In the 1960s, the Chinese government created a set of rules for sanda, making it both a sport and a martial art. In modern sanda, fighters can use their elbows, knees, fists, and feet to take an opponent to the floor. However, they are not allowed to target their opponent's throat or joints.

People from all over the world practice sanda. These two fighters are from Russia (red) and Iran (black).

The difference between a sport and a martial art is how dangerous it is to the fighters. When sanda became a sport, the rules were changed to make it less violent. In a real fight, a person would use martial arts to defend themselves against someone who wants to seriously hurt them, so none of these rules apply.

Although there is no doubt that sanda is a Chinese martial art, it has been influenced over time by Western fighting styles. Sanda is now common in mixed martial arts (MMA) competitions. These allow fighters to use moves from all different kinds of martial arts. Additionally, as knowledge and science have advanced over the years, some parts of sanda have changed. For example, sanda fighters of the past didn't wear protective gear such as helmets and gloves. Today, to keep everyone safe, they do.

MMA can be very dangerous, even for professionals.

Martial Arts in Film

The first time many people outside of China learned about kung fu, it was through movies. Bruce Lee—one of the most beloved martial artists in history—helped make martial arts movies popular. He starred in movies such as *Fist of Fury* and *Enter the Dragon* in the early 1970s.

In 1973, *Five Fingers of Death*—the first kung fu movie to be shown in the United States—opened in New York City. Audiences went wild and demanded more, and kung fu movies have been popular in America ever since.

Lee was born in San Francisco in 1940, and his parents gave him the name Lee Jun Fan. He was given the American name Bruce by a nurse at the hospital in San Francisco where he was born. He lived in both China and the United States during his lifetime. He studied kung fu under Ip Man and became a wing chun teacher in the 1960s.

Through his movies, he inspired many other famous fighters, including Sugar Ray Leonard and Mike Tyson. Dana White, the president of an MMA **promotion** company called the Ultimate Fighting Championship (UFC), called Lee "the father of MMA." Sadly, Lee died in 1973 at the age of 32, likely due to side effects from medication he was taking.

This Rwandan stamp from 2010 that features Bruce Lee shows that he remains popular around the world decades after his death.

Even some non-Chinese actors have become famous for kung fu. Chuck Norris and Jean-Claude Van Damme are two movie stars who have become well-known for their kung fu skills.

Jackie Chan is another famous martial arts star. Born Chan Kong-sang in Hong Kong, he found work at a young age as an actor and **stuntman**. In the late 1970s, a movie producer named Lo Wei cast Chan in several movies, hoping he would be the next Bruce Lee. Although Chan did become incredibly famous, he never tried to act in dramatic roles the way Lee did. Instead, he used comedy with his martial arts skills. As of 2022, Chan has worked on more than 200 movies and is a beloved actor around the world.

Martial arts movies continue to be popular worldwide. Recently, Marvel's *Shang-Chi*, starring Simu Liu, and *Everything Everywhere All at Once*, starring Michelle Yeoh, gained a lot of positive attention from fans and critics.

Michelle Yeoh is a movie star who has used styles such as wing chun and tai chi in her movies. She is best known for her roles in *Crouching Tiger, Hidden Dragon* and *Everything Everywhere All at Once*.

Don't Get It Twisted!

There are a lot of martial arts in the world, and a lot of them are not Chinese. However, people often get these martial arts mixed up. Here is a brief overview of some popular martial arts that aren't Chinese and therefore do not fall under the "kung fu" umbrella.

Many people have heard of a dojo, but fewer have heard of a kwoon. These are both buildings where martial arts are practiced. A dojo is for Japanese martial arts, and a kwoon is for Chinese martial arts.

- **Karate** is a well-known Japanese martial art. Practitioners wear white outfits with colored belts that show their level of skill. In order from beginner to expert, the colors are white, orange, blue, yellow, green, brown, and black. A practitioner must have each belt for a certain amount of time before they are allowed to try for the next belt. The main difference between karate and kung fu fighting styles is that karate focuses more on offensive strikes, while kung fu focuses more on defensive strikes. However, karate practitioners are taught never to start a fight and only to use their skills if they are being attacked.

■ **Krav Maga** was developed in Czechoslovakia in the 1930s. Its creator, Imi Lichtenfeld, taught it to Czechoslovakian Jews to help them defend themselves from the Nazis. When Israel became a country in 1948, Lichtenfeld taught Krav Maga to its military. In the 1980s, it spread to the United States. Today, there are Krav Maga schools all over the world. Unlike most Chinese martial arts, Krav Maga is used only for self-defense, not for show in tournaments.

■ **Taekwondo** is a Korean martial art that was developed about 2,000 years ago. Like many Chinese martial arts today, taekwondo is both a self-defense system and a sport. It was brought to the United States in the 1950s by Korean instructors and quickly gained popularity. In 1988, it became an Olympic sport.

Taekwondo and karate are popular after-school activities for children of all ages and genders. The outfits look very similar.

Glossary

accuracy: Having the ability to hit an intended target.
acrobatics: Difficult or dangerous stunts that require skillful control of the body.
biennially: Happening every two years.
brutal: Cruel and harsh.
Buddhism: A religion of eastern and central Asia based on the teachings of Siddhartha Gautama.
characterize: To be a typical or distinguishing quality of something.
consciously: Known or felt by a person's inner self.
ethics: The discipline dealing with what is good and bad and with moral duty and obligation.
meditation: The act or an instance of planning or thinking quietly.
mobility: The ability to move freely.
monastery: A place where a community of monks lives and works.
philosophy: A set of ideas about how to do something or how to live.
promotion: The act of helping something happen, develop, or increase.
reflex: An action or movement that is made automatically without thinking as a reaction to a stimulus.
self-confidence: Someone's confidence in themselves and in their own abilities.
stuntman: Someone who performs an unusual or difficult act.
systematized: To arrange according to a definite plan.

For More Information

6 Dragons Kung Fu Free Course
www.6dragonskungfu.com/complete-course-kung-fu-online-free
This website offers a free video kung fu course so people can try it at home before deciding if they want to pay for in-person classes.

Britannica Kids: Martial Art
kids.britannica.com/students/article/martial-art/275710
This article explains the differences between martial arts from around the world.

Chinese Martial Arts Museum
tripstoshanghai.com/attractions/show/chinese_martial_arts_museum.htm
This museum in Shanghai includes displays of weapons, videos of martial artists, and more.

Encyclopedia.com: Chinese Martial Arts
www.encyclopedia.com/environment/encyclopedias-almanacs-transcripts-and-maps/martial-arts-chinese-martial-arts
Read more about the history and modern practice of Chinese martial arts.

Kiddle: Chinese Martial Arts
kids.kiddle.co/Chinese_martial_arts
Read more about Chinese martial arts and take a look at some cool photos.

Martial Arts History Museum
martialartsmuseum.com
This martial arts museum is in Los Angeles, California. It features exhibits from cultures around the world, including China.

Wing Chun Online
www.wingchunonline.com/resources
This website includes free articles about the history of wing chun, videos of practitioners, and even plans for how to build a wooden practice dummy at home.

YouTube: 36,000 Kids You Don't Want to Mess With
www.youtube.com/watch?v=3FDL4ZYEfcw
Students at the largest martial arts school in China, the Shaolin Temple Kung Fu Academy, show off their skills.

YouTube: Bruce Lee—Fist of Fury
www.youtube.com/watch?v=y9PkOR7kCrQ
Watch Bruce Lee fight in one of his most famous roles.

For Further Reading

Casarella, Antonello, and Roberto Ghetti. *A Complete Guide to Kung Fu.* New York, NY: Enslow Publishing, 2018.

Cheong, Jack, and Laurel Teo. *Origins of Chinese Martial Arts.* Singapore: ASIAPAC Books, 2002.

Giang, Kristen Mai, and Alina Chau. *The Rise (and Falls) of Jackie Chan.* New York, NY: Crown Books for Young Readers, 2022.

Gigliotti, Jim, and John Hinderlighter. *Who Was Bruce Lee?* New York, NY: Grossett & Dunlap, 2014.

Howell, Brian. *Kung Fu.* Minneapolis, MN: SportsZone/Abdo Publishing, 2015.

Johnson, Nathan J. *Kung Fu.* Broomall, PA: Mason Crest, 2015.

Lorini, Walter. *A Complete Guide to Tai Chi.* New York, NY: Enslow Publishing, 2018.

Meister, Cari. *Martial Arts Fun.* North Mankato, MN: Pebble, 2021.

Peterson, Susan Lynn. *Legends of the Martial Arts Masters: Tales of Bravery and Adventure Featuring Bruce Lee, Jackie Chan and Other Great Martial Artists.* Tokyo, Japan: Tuttle Publishing, 2019.

Shaffer, Jody Jensen, and Gregory Copeland. *Who Is Jackie Chan?* New York, NY: Penguin Workshop, 2020.

Tsai, Chi-Chung, and Brian Bruya. *The Tao Speaks: Lao-Tzu's Whispers of Wisdom.* New York, NY: Anchor Books, 1995.

Wilson, Sierra. *Tai Chi.* New York, NY: AV2, 2021.

World Book, Inc. *Famous Myths and Legends of the World: Myths and Legends of China.* Chicago, IL: World Book, 2015.

Bibliography

"History of Shuai Jiao." Traditional Wing Chun Kung Fu Academy, North American Headquarters. 2012. http://traditionalwingchun.com/twckf/history-of-shuai-jiao/.

Meredith, Anne. *"The Who, What and Why of Chinese Martial Arts."* Chinese Language Institute. January 9, 2022. https://studycli.org/chinese-culture/chinese-martial-arts/.

"What Was the First Martial Art?" Get into Martial Arts. 2022. https://www.getintomartialarts.com/what-was-the-first-martial-art/.

The Editors of Encyclopaedia Britannica. *"Huangdi."* Encyclopaedia Britannica. February 14, 2018. https://www.britannica.com/topic/Huangdi.

martial. *"MMA—North vs. South Kung Fu."* Martial Tribes. June 17, 2018. www.martialtribes.com/north-vs-south-kung-fu.

Naumann, Sara. *"A Brief History of Shaolin Temple."* TripSavvy. January 21, 2019. https://www.tripsavvy.com/brief-history-shaolin-temple-1495708.

"History of Wing Chun." International Wing Chun Academy. Accessed September 20, 2022. https://www.wingchun.edu.au/wing-chun/history.

"Behind the First Gold Medal: Wushu Changquan Explained." CGTN. August 20, 2018. https://news.cgtn.com/news/3d3d514d30496a4e79457a6333566d54/share_p.html.

Frantzis, Bruce. *"Bagua Circle Walking."* Energy Arts. July 25, 2010. https://www.energyarts.com/bagua-circle-walking/.

"Baguazhang." New World Encyclopedia. Accessed September 20, 2022. https://www.newworldencyclopedia.org/entry/Baguazhang.

"A Brief Introduction of Wushu Sanda." Arizona Sanda Association. Accessed September 20, 2022. https://azsanda.org/sanda/.

Biography.com Editors. *"Bruce Lee Biography."* Biography.com. May 24, 2021. https://www.biography.com/actor/bruce-lee.

The Editors of Encyclopaedia Britannica. *"Jackie Chan."* Encyclopaedia Britannica. August 16, 2022. https://www.britannica.com/biography/Jackie-Chan.

Anuradha. *"What Is the Difference Between Karate and Kung Fu."* PEDIAA. April 27, 2022. https://pediaa.com/what-is-the-difference-between-karate-and-kung-fu/.

Index

A
acrobatics, 13, 26
Asian Games, 29

B
baguazhang, 30, 31, 33
Bodhidharma, 14
Buddhism, 14, 17, 22

C
Chan, Jackie (Chan Kong-sang), 41
changquan, 26, 27, 28, 29
Chen Wang Ting, 18, 19
Crouching Tiger, Hidden Dragon, 41

E
Enter the Dragon, 38
Everything Everywhere All at Once, 41
exercise, 4, 14, 17, 21, 22, 30, 33
external, 10, 18, 26

F
Fist of Fury, 38
Five Fingers of Death, 38

I
internal, 10, 18, 30
Ip Man, 22, 24, 25, 38

J
Jiao Li (Jiao Ti), 6, 7
judo, 34

K
karate, 42, 43
kickboxing, 34
Krav Maga, 43
kung fu, 13, 14, 15, 16, 22, 23, 38, 42
Kung Fu Panda, 17

L
Lee, Bruce (Lee Jun Fan), 22, 38, 39, 41
Leonard, Sugar Ray, 39
Lichtenfeld, Imi, 43
Lim, Joanna, 31
Liu, Simu, 41

M
military, 6, 7, 9, 13, 17, 19, 43
mixed martial arts (MMA), 34, 36, 37, 39
movies, 17, 38, 39, 40, 41

N
Norris, Chuck, 41
northern style, 12, 13, 26

O
Olympics, 29, 43

S
sanda, 34, 35, 37
Shang-Chi, 41
Shaolin kung fu, 14, 15, 16, 17, 18, 26
Shaolin Temple, 14, 15, 22
Shuai Jiao, 8, 9, 14
southern style, 13

T
taekwondo, 43
Tai Chi, 18, 19, 20, 21, 30, 41
Taoism, 18, 19, 30
Taoist circle walking, 30
Tyson, Mike, 39

V
Van Damme, Jean-Claude, 41

W
weapons, 4, 9, 21, 25, 27, 32, 33
Wing Chun, 22, 23, 24, 25, 31, 38, 41

Y
Yeoh, Michelle, 40, 41
yinyang, 10, 11, 18